# Louis Pasteur

## YOUNG SCIENTIST

by Francene Sabin
illustrated by Susan Swan

**Troll Associates**

*Library of Congress Cataloging in Publication Data*

Sabin, Francene.
   Louis Pasteur, young scientist.

   Summary: Traces the childhood and young adult years
of the renowned French microbiologist whose interest in
chemistry resulted in the process called pasteurization.
      1. Pasteur, Louis, 1822-1895—Juvenile literature.
2. Scientists—France—Biography—Juvenile literature.
[1. Pasteur, Louis, 1822-1895.   2. Scientists]
I. Swan, Susan Elizabeth, ill.   II. Title.
Q143.P2S24   1983      591.2 '322 '0924   [B]   [92]      82-15924
ISBN 0-89375-853-1
ISBN 0-89375-854-X (pbk.)

# Louis Pasteur

## YOUNG SCIENTIST

FORGERON

In the early 1800s, the town of Arbois, France, was very much like little towns everywhere. There was a long road that ran from one end of the village to the other. A number of small streets crossed it. On the main street, facing the town square, was the church. On the other side of the square was the Arbois town hall, a handsome stone building.

There were just a few shops in Arbois. One was the bootmaker's. Another was the blacksmith's. Next to the blacksmith's was the livery stable, filled with horses and carriages. People who needed to travel to another town on business or to attend a wedding or funeral rented a horse and carriage at the stable.

On the same street was the chemist's shop. The chemist was a very special man to the people of Arbois. He sold pills and cough syrups and skin creams, just as a modern druggist does. But he did things that druggists don't have to do today. He had to make all of the medicines he sold. Some he made by mixing chemical powders. And some he made from herbs that grew in the fields and mountains near the town. He even went out and collected the herbs himself.

There was a little boy in Arbois who visited the chemist's shop almost every day. The quiet five-year-old, little Louis Pasteur, would stand for hours next to the chemist's marble worktable. He loved to watch the man make his medicines and creams. There were plant roots to grind fine as dust. There were liquids of different colors to mix and pour into bottles. Then the chemist would make a label for each bottle and write an important-looking Latin name on it.

Louis also listened to the customers who came into the chemist's shop. They told the man about their aches and pains, or about their sick farm animals. The chemist listened, nodded his head, asked questions, and told the customers to come back the next day. Then he made up some kind of medicine for the customer.

This was the part Louis enjoyed most of all. It was like spying on a magician. Some chemicals went *poof!* when the chemist heated them over a small flame. There were liquids that bubbled and changed color. And smells that were so strong and strange. It was a mysterious world, and Louis wanted to know everything about it.

On some days, while the chemist worked, he talked to Louis. "I do what I can to help people," the man said. "But disease..." He shrugged his shoulders. "Disease is hard to fight. It comes from nowhere—right out of the air. One day a cow is well, the next day it is very sick, even dead. It is the same with people. Sometimes they get better, sometimes they don't."

10

Louis Pasteur did not say much. But he watched and listened to the chemist, as he did to everything that went on around him. He was a serious little boy. He had been that way almost from the day he was born, December 27, 1822. Back then, the Pasteur family lived in the town of Dôle, a few miles from Arbois. But after Louis and his two little sisters were born, the Pasteurs needed a bigger house. And there was no other house in Dôle that was just right for Mr. Pasteur's trade.

Louis's father, Jean-Joseph Pasteur, was a tanner. He made beautiful leather out of animal skins. It took a lot of water to do this. That meant a tanner had to live next to a river. When the Pasteurs did not find a large enough house on the river in Dôle, they decided to move to another town. They found the perfect place in Arbois, right on the bank of the Cuisance River.

12

The new house was three stories high. There was a small garden in front and a large dirt courtyard in back. Around three sides of the property was a high stone wall. On the fourth side was the fast-flowing river. Louis and his sisters liked to sit on the bank of the river and fish in the silvery waters.

Louis also liked to watch his father at work in the tannery, which was in the Pasteur home. In the cellar, Mr. Pasteur kept huge bins of salt. When fresh sheep and cattle skins arrived, he put them in the bins and covered them with salt. The salt dried the skins and kept them from rotting.

"Why do skins rot if you don't use salt?" Louis asked.

"I don't know. Nobody knows," his father answered. "Some people say that the night air rots the skins. Some say it is caused by heat or cold. And some say it is the way things are, and we must not question it."

"Do other things spoil the same way?" Louis wanted to know.

13

Mr. Pasteur stopped working and sat down on a stool. He was pleased that his son was bright and wanted to learn things. Mr. Pasteur had a dream for Louis. The boy would get a good education. He would become a wise man, even a teacher. This meant a lot to Mr. Pasteur, who had very little education himself.

"Many things go bad," he told the boy. "One day milk is fresh and sweet, the next day it is sour. One day meat is fine, the next day it can make you sick. This happens with grapes, too. Mister DuPont had that problem in his vineyard last year. Some of the wine he made was very good. But some of it was bitter, and some was sharp as vinegar.

"From one day to the next," Mr. Pasteur went on, "the dairy farmer and the grape grower do not know what will happen. And our cheeses and wines bring riches and glory to France. So it is a sad time—and a poor one—when these things go bad."

In his most grown-up voice, Louis said, "Someday I will find out why these things happen and stop them. I will help the dairy farmer and the grape grower. I will do something good for France!"

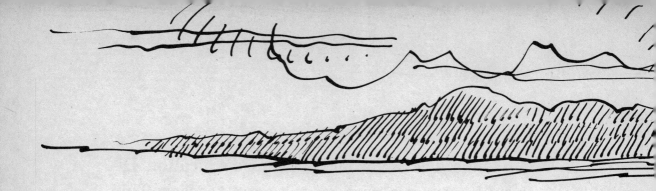

Mr. Pasteur smiled at his little boy. He was glad that Louis had dreams of doing great things with his life. "If you believe in yourself and study hard," Mr. Pasteur said, "*anything* is possible." Then he patted the boy's head and went back to work.

Mr. Pasteur would have liked to talk longer with his son. But a tanner had so much to do. After the skins were kept for a while in the salt bins, they were taken out for cleaning. Using a stiff brush, Mr. Pasteur scraped off all the fur until the skins were smooth. Next, he put the skins into the tanning pits in the courtyard. Each of these pits was wide and deep.

At the bottom of a pit, Mr. Pasteur spread a layer of oak-bark chips. On top of that he spread some skins. Then he put on more layers of chips and skins, until the pit was completely filled. After this, he filled buckets with water from the nearby river and poured it into the pit.

These skins were not touched for a year. In that time, the water took a chemical called tannin out of the oak bark. This tannin turned the skins a rich brown. It also strengthened the skins so that they would not fall apart or tear easily.

When the year was over, Mr. Pasteur took the skins out of the pit. He rinsed them in the river for a day or two. Then he hung them out to dry. As soon as they were dry, he pounded the skins until they were soft and rubbed them with oil.

17

Louis and his friends liked to see Mr. Pasteur at his work. They would often gather to watch him or to play in the Pasteurs' workshop. Lying all about were scraps of beautiful, soft leather. Out of these scraps, the children would make leather pouches and slingshots.

Mr. Pasteur enjoyed the company of Louis and his friends. Although there never seemed to be an end to his back-breaking, dirty work, it was all worth it. Mr. Pasteur told his wife, "The money we save will bring our children an education. And that will bring them a better way of life."

On Louis's first day of school, Mr. Pasteur was as excited as his son. He made sure that six-year-old Louis had his brand-new notebook and his freshly cut quill pen. He straightened the bow tie Louis wore with his new blue wool school uniform.

When Louis was ready to leave, Mrs. Pasteur gave him his lunch bag. In it was a thick slice of cheese, a chunk of sausage, a piece of home-baked bread, and an apple. Louis kissed his mother good-by and looked eagerly at his father, who was dressed in his best Sunday clothing. And off father and son went, hand-in-hand, to the first-grade class at the local school for boys.

Mr. Pasteur waved good-by to Louis at the school gate and returned home to work. Louis saw his best friend, Jules Vercel, and ran to join him. They went into their classroom and took seats next to each other. There were a lot of boys in the class. Some were first-graders, like Louis and Jules. Others were a year or two older, and they were in second or third grade.

21

There was one room and one teacher for the three grades. But one teacher could not teach all three grades at one time. So he had some of the smartest third-graders help him. They were called monitors. Each monitor was in charge of six first-graders. The monitor showed the students what work they should do. Then he went back to his own desk. The teacher walked around the room, checking the work of each boy and making corrections when he had to.

Louis wished he could be a monitor someday. He wanted his parents to be proud of him. He worked very hard on his lessons. Every letter he wrote had to look just right. When he did addition and subtraction, his numbers had to be perfectly neat and in very straight rows.

Louis took so much time doing his arithmetic and his spelling that the teacher got the wrong idea about him. "The boy works very hard. And he is very well behaved," the teacher told Mr. and Mrs. Pasteur. "But I'm afraid Louis will not come to much. He is a bit slow to learn."

His parents did not give up hope for Louis's future. They knew he was much smarter than the teacher thought. Every night, Mr. Pasteur sat with Louis and went over his lessons. The boy read a page out loud, then they talked about it. Mr. Pasteur gave Louis simple arithmetic problems and praised the boy for each one he got right.

Mrs. Pasteur paid close attention to Louis's drawing. She bought him a new set of crayons, and she hung up every picture he made. The drawings were very good. Louis looked at things quite carefully, and thought a long time before doing anything with the crayons. That was why he was a "slow" student, and also why he drew so well.

Before Louis made a picture of a butterfly, he watched the way it flew, the way its wings folded at rest, and the way its feelers curved. Then, when he drew the butterfly, every detail was exactly right.

This talent for careful observation, which he showed at such a young age, was to become very important in Louis Pasteur's life. Years later, when he became a scientist, he would use this talent to study and draw what he saw through the microscope. His drawings of yeasts, mold spores, and other microscopic life are so good that scientists today can tell exactly which microbe each drawing shows.

But life wasn't all books and work for Louis. Every week he visited his friend, the chemist. Louis looked at all the herbs, roots, and minerals the man had collected. The boy asked how they were used and where they came from. Then he made ink drawings of these things, and colored them at home with crayons.

On other days, Louis and Jules Vercel went fishing for trout in the Cuisance River. They had a favorite spot where it was always quiet. One summer day in 1831, while they were fishing there, the boys heard screams. Seconds later they saw Annette Ledoux, the little girl who lived next door to the Pasteurs. She was running and crying, "A wolf bit me! A wolf bit me! Help! Please help!"

Louis and Jules dropped their fishing poles and caught up with Annette. They saw bite marks on her leg. "Don't worry, Annette," Louis said. "We will take you home." And the three children ran back to the village.

While Jules took Annette to her house, Louis went to get the doctor. Louis knew that Annette was in great danger. Eight people in Arbois had already died after being bitten by a wolf. The animal was sick with rabies, a deadly disease caused by a virus. Sometimes an animal with rabies will go mad and bite other animals and people. In those days, nobody knew what caused rabies, and there was no way to keep animals from getting it.

Louis and the doctor hurried to the Ledoux house. There, the doctor pressed a red-hot iron on the little girl's wounds. It was a painful treatment, and it usually didn't help, anyway. Still, it was the only thing the doctor knew to do.

Annette was very lucky—she lived. Most rabies' victims did not.

31

Louis wanted to know more about rabies. "Where does it come from?" he asked the doctor, the chemist, the teachers at school—anyone who might have an answer. We do not know, they told him. An animal gets sick for no reason. Then it makes people sick. That is all there is to know.

These answers were not good enough for Louis. Something caused rabies. And somebody should find out what it was. Only then, Louis was sure, would there be a way to stop it. There must be people somewhere who could solve this riddle. Louis thought about this a lot.

At the age of thirteen, Louis entered the Arbois high school. He still did his work very slowly and carefully. But now it won him high marks and praise from his teachers. He was never the first one finished with a test, but he almost always had every answer right.

Mr. Romanet, the high-school principal, soon noticed the hard-working, intelligent youngster. One day, he asked Louis to come to his office. "What do you plan to do after high school?" the principal asked.

Louis thought for a moment. "People say my drawings are good," he said. "Maybe I can be an artist."

"Have you ever thought of becoming a teacher?" Mr. Romanet asked.

"That would be wonderful, and it would make my parents so happy," Louis said. "But to become a teacher I would have to go to college. And I don't know if I'm smart enough."

"You are. And if you study hard, you can be anything you want to be. Even a university professor!" Mr. Romanet said. "I will help you in any way I can. Let me speak to your father about this. We will decide what is the best thing to do."

Mr. Romanet and Mr. Pasteur talked about the teenager's future. They agreed that Louis should continue at the Arbois high school for two more years. Then, he should spend a year at a fine private high school in Paris. That would help him get ready to take the difficult college entrance test.

In October 1838, Louis left Arbois for Paris. He had never been away from home alone before this. He was scared and near tears. There was only one thing that kept him from jumping off the stage-coach and running home. His best friend, Jules Vercel, was also going to the Paris school. The two boys would be living in the same house.

Even so, from the minute the coach left Arbois, Louis was miserable. The trip to Paris took forty-eight hours. There were no seats inside the coach, so the boys had to sit outside, huddled under a blanket. It rained the whole time. The boys were soaked and shivering long before they got to Paris.

It was a bad start, and things got worse for Louis. He tried to study, but he was too homesick to keep his mind on his books. He could not eat or sleep. "If I could just get one whiff of the tannery yard," he moaned to Jules, "then I think I would be all right."

The principal of the school in Paris, Mr. Barbet, saw how sad Louis was. If things continue this way, he told himself, the boy will become ill. So he wrote to Mr. Pasteur, suggesting that Louis be taken home.

A few days later, a classmate came to Louis's room. "There's someone downstairs to see you," the boy said.

Louis started down the stairs slowly. Then he saw who his visitor was and raced down the rest of the way. "Oh, Papa! I'm so happy to see you!"

"I have come to take you home," Mr. Pasteur said gently. "We all miss you very much."

Back in Arbois, Louis returned to the local high school. He was worried that his parents were disappointed in him, even though they said nothing. He told this to Mr. Romanet. "You are not a failure," the principal answered. "We all agree that it was *our* mistake to send you away too soon. When you are ready, you will go away to college. All things come in their right time."

Louis felt better about himself after this talk. He finished that year with the highest marks in his class. And he also set to work on many new drawings. He especially liked to draw portraits of his family, friends, and neighbors. Carefully observing his subject, young Louis used beautiful pastel colors to capture the mood and features of the person sitting before him.

Louis's parents soon arranged for him to go to a better high school. It was in Besançon, only thirty miles from Arbois. This was a fine idea, Louis thought. Mr. Pasteur visited the town on business once every month. That meant Louis would see his father often. The teenager also was close enough to come home for a weekend, if he felt homesick. And now, two years older than when he went to Paris, Louis felt ready to leave home.

Louis plunged into his studies at the new school. Along with his regular classes, he took science lessons from a chemist. And he continued with his painting. At the end of his first year in Besançon, eighteen-year-old Louis wrote his parents, "I hold a steady place among the best students in my classes. But I hope my standing will be even better within a few months."

During his second year, he was given a job as assistant teacher of the younger boys. For this he was paid a small amount of money and given a free room and meals. At the end of the year, he graduated with honors in mathematics, physics, and Latin, and was given a prize for drawing. Now it was time to take the test for college.

Louis passed the tough entrance test to the excellent Teachers' College in Paris. Only he was not satisfied with his mark. Twenty-two young men were accepted. Of that group, Louis was fifteenth on the list. "I can't accept a place in the class," he told his parents. "I know I can do better!"

One more year of hard studying gave Louis the preparation he needed. This time, when he took the entrance test, he came out fourth best in all of France. Now, he felt, he was ready to go to college and be a top student.

Louis was right. He did very well, especially in science. Even before he finished school, Pasteur's work in the laboratory—a study of chemical crystals—won him the attention of scientists the world over.

But the young man was just beginning. Soon after, he became the university professor his parents had dreamed he would be. And, in the years that followed, he did things that not even they could have dreamed. Louis made discoveries that changed the course of history. He never lost the curiosity he had felt as a child, wanting to know why milk spoiled, why grapes in the vineyard rotted, and where disease came from. He could not believe the answers that others accepted—that these things just happened, and that there was no other reason.

In the same careful way he had always worked, Pasteur looked for the answers. He used the microscope and every other laboratory tool. He ran test after test. He kept very careful records of every test he made. And he finally found the answers to many of his questions.

Why did milk spoil? Because of a microscopic life form called bacteria. Why did grapes rot? Bacteria. And what caused disease? Bacteria. Today we know much about the microscopic world of bacteria. But in the middle of the nineteenth century, this was a stunning idea. And many people found it hard to believe—until Pasteur gave them proof. This is what the great scientist showed them. If you look at spoiled milk through a microscope, you will see many bacteria cells. But if you look at unspoiled milk, you will see very few bacteria cells. Then he showed that heating milk kept it fresh—and free of bacteria—for a long time. This discovery—called pasteurization—made Louis a hero.

For pasteurization alone, Louis would be remembered forever. But before he died, on September 28, 1895, he discovered far more. After endless hours of laboratory work and hundreds of tests, he developed a vaccine to prevent rabies. Then he developed another vaccine to prevent anthrax, a disease that attacks cattle, sheep, and people.

Because of Pasteur's pioneering work in vaccination, a new science came to be. This science—using the microbes that cause a disease to fight that same disease—was born in Louis's laboratory. Today, vaccines protect us against polio, tuberculosis, diptheria, smallpox, measles, and many other diseases. And it all began with the curiosity of a small, quiet boy in the little town of Arbois, France.